GROSS STUFF UNDERWATER

BY PAM ROSENBERG

ILLUSTRATED BY BEATRIZ HELENA RAMOS

ABOUT THE AUTHOR:

Pam Rosenberg lives in Illinois with a husband, two kids, two cats, a hermit crab, a few bugs, and lots of bacteria and other tiny things she doesn't like to think about.

ABOUT THE ILLUSTRATOR:

Beatriz Helena Ramos is an artist from Venezuela who lives and plays in NYC. She works from her animation studio, Dancing Diablo, where she directs animated spots. Beatriz has illustrated a dozen books and she particularly loves gross stories.

The Child's World

Published by The Child's World®
1980 Lookout Drive • Mankato, MN 56003-1705
800-599-READ • www.childsworld.com

Photos: Natursports/Dreamstime.com: 13;
Rattiya Thongdumhyu/Shutterstock.com: cover, 8

ISBN 9781503850262 (Reinforced Library Binding)
ISBN 9781503850743 (Portable Document Format)
ISBN 9781503851504 (Online Multi-user eBook)
LCCN: 2021930089

Printed in the United States of America

TABLE OF CONTENTS

AHHHHH. SWIMMING! IT'S A GREAT WARM-WEATHER PASTIME.

You can even swim indoors when it's cold outside if you have an indoor pool nearby. Some people enjoy splashing around in all that nice, cool water. Others like to jump in and swim for exercise. Still others like to participate in water sports such as surfing and polo. Would you like to learn more about what lives under the surface of all that water before you decide whether to take the plunge? Then dive into the pages of this book—if you dare!!

PUTRID POOLS

When you jump into a swimming pool for a nice, refreshing swim, keep in mind that you share that water with all of the other people swimming in the pool. And **wherever there are people, there are germs.** Most germs are harmless, but some of them can make you sick. One common illness that can be spread by swimming pool water is diarrhea. That's one of the reasons your mom and dad always tell you not to swallow the pool water!

Need another reason to keep the pool water out of your mouth? **Just think of the swimming pool as a big bathtub.** All of the dirt and sweat on everyone's body is washed off in the water. Would you drink the water from your bathtub after you or one of your family members took a bath? I didn't think so!

RANCID RIVERS

Did you ever think about what happens to all that water when it rains? Sure, some of it soaks into the ground, but what about the water that doesn't soak in? As it runs along the ground, it picks up all kinds of stuff. Stuff like **fertilizers**, **pesticides**, trash, and animal poop. So it isn't just rainwater that runs into rivers and other bodies of water. Makes the thought of swimming in them just a little less appealing, doesn't it?

The Amazon River is home to electric eels. They live in murky waters where it is difficult to see anything. They give off a kind of **electricity** and surround themselves with a force field. That way they can sense when something is near them and move around in the dark water without crashing into rocks or other fish. Electric eels can also use their electricity to stun prey. In fact, they can send out a 500-**volt** shock that is **strong enough to knock over a large mammal** standing in shallow water. Do you know any large mammals? Here's a hint: Look in a mirror.

LOATHSOME LAKES

Try not to swallow the water. If you do, you might be eating lots of living things. **Plankton** are microscopic plants and animals that live in water and float along with the currents. A big gulp of lake water could contain thousands of them!

Lampreys are strange fish. They look a lot like swimming worms. A lamprey has a round mouth with razor-sharp teeth. Its tongue also has teeth. When a fish or an unlucky swimmer comes too close to a lamprey, the lamprey attacks. It attaches its mouth to the victim and its sharp teeth gnaw through the victim's skin. **Then the lamprey uses its sharp tongue to lick up the victim's blood.** It lets go after it's full. Then the wounded fish—or human—swims away. A fish won't die from a lamprey bite, but the wound often gets infected. Many fish die from infected lamprey bites. People unlucky enough to be bitten by a lamprey don't die, they're just grossed out!

Leeches are a kind of worm. They have a special mouth that attaches to another animal and sucks the animal's blood for a tasty meal. One kind of leech that lives in the lakes and streams in southern Europe, northern Africa, and the Middle East **can enter your body in drinking water**. If you drink one in your water, it will attach itself to the lining of your nose or throat and may eventually end up in your lungs!

OOZING OCEANS

Did you know that oceans cover about 71% of Earth's surface? About 97% of the water on Earth is contained in oceans. Just imagine how much icky stuff there must be in that much water!

Sharks are one of the dangers many people think about when they think about swimming in an ocean. There are more than 450 different kinds of sharks. Most of them are not a danger to humans. **But try not to get anywhere near a great white shark.** These monsters can grow to 20 feet (6 meters) long and have been known to attack humans. They have about 3,000 teeth and like to eat!

Blue whales are the largest mammals on Earth. **They are probably the largest animals that have ever lived on Earth.** They are about 90 to 100 feet (27.5 to 30.5 m) long and can weigh more than 100 tons (99,800 kilograms). A blue whale's heart is about the size of a Volkswagen Beetle automobile and weighs about 1,000 pounds (454 kilograms)! But you don't have to worry about being eaten by one of these giants. They feed on tiny shrimp-like animals called **krill**. They can eat up to 40 million of these creatures a day.

Be careful not to get too close to a moray eel. Morays grow to be about 5 feet (1.5 m) long. They have very sharp teeth and **when they bite something, they don't let go.** If you are bitten by a moray eel, the only way to get it off of you is to cut off its head and break its jaws!

Hagfish might be the grossest animal in the oceans. They are also known as slime eels. That's because they are completely covered by **mucus**. The mucus oozes out of about ninety holes called **pores** that line the body of a hagfish. When a hagfish wants to avoid a **predator**, it oozes out streams of thick, gooey mucus. Another gross feature of hagfish? A hagfish has one tooth on the roof of its mouth and a tongue that has two rows of sharp teeth. Its mouth is surrounded by four pairs of **tentacles**. When a hagfish eats, it gets inside the body of another fish and eats the fish from the inside out. It eats the guts and flesh, leaving nothing but skin and bones.

Lots of people think that sea stars—often called starfish—are kind of cute. And they are if you like an animal with rows and rows of little tube feet, a mouth on the bottom of its body, and its **anus** (the hole where it poops from) on the top of its body. Sea stars have an unusual way of eating. **They push their stomachs outside of their bodies and digest their food.** Then they tuck their tummies back in. Imagine what it would look like at dinnertime if your family ate that way!

Sea cucumbers are leathery-skinned animals that live on the sea floor. They are called sea cucumbers because they look a lot like the cucumbers you buy in your grocery store. They have tentacles that ooze mucus to help them trap food. But that's not the most disgusting feature of a sea cucumber. **When this creature is threatened, it shoots its guts out of its body.** The predator gets confused by the gooey **intestines** that look kind of like cooked spaghetti noodles. That gives the sea cucumber time to get away. But don't worry. The sea cucumber doesn't die without its guts; it just grows new ones!

Octopuses are odd-looking animals with eight arms. When an octopus feels threatened—usually by a sea lion, otter, or seal that wants a meal—**it squirts out a lot of dark brownish-black ink.** The ink clouds the water so the hungry animal can't see the octopus. The ink makes it hard for the animal to smell the octopus, too. Most octopuses are shy and harmless, but look out for the Australian blue-ringed octopus. This small (about the size of a golf ball) octopus has a deadly bite. The bite of the blue-ringed octopus is painless, but its **venom** can kill an adult human being in minutes!

The sting of a jellyfish is extremely painful. These see-through clumps that float in the ocean have long tentacles. One tentacle can have millions of stingers. The stingers of most jellyfish are too small to get through human skin. But one large jellyfish that can hurt humans is the box jelly, sometimes called a sea wasp. When a box jelly is full grown, it is about as big as a basketball and its tentacles—up to sixty of them—can be as much as 15 feet (4.6 meters) long. Try to keep away from those long tentacles.

The sting of a box jellyfish can kill a person!

While most animals, humans included, try to stay away from jellyfish, **sea turtles search them out.** Jellyfish are one of their favorite foods. The turtles are able to eat the jellyfish and their venom with no harmful effects.

Blowfish have a great way to keep predators away. When they are threatened, they swallow water and make themselves twice as big as normal. Not only are they big, but they are also prickly. Think of a Koosh ball all blown up and ready to burst.

Many kinds of blowfish are also loaded with poison. **So, what kind of animal would think about eating these prickly, poisonous fish? Humans, that's who!** Yes, believe it or not, in Japan they call it *fugu*, and it is considered a rare **delicacy**. People pay a lot of money to eat the stuff. Chefs are specially trained to serve this dangerous dish. But if they make a mistake and don't prepare the fish correctly, the person who eats it may die!

As you might have figured out from the blowfish information, one person's gross is another person's special treat. **Next time you're near a body of water, take a closer look beneath the surface.** What you find there may fascinate you or gross you out. Or maybe a little of both!

GLOSSARY

anus (AY-nuhs) The anus is the exterior opening at the end of your digestive tract. The anus of a sea star is on top of its body.

delicacy (DEL-uh-kuh-see) A delicacy is something that is very delicious to eat and is considered to be a very special treat. Blowfish is a delicacy in Japan.

electricity (i-lek-TRISS-uh-tee) Electricity is a form of energy created by the movement of electrons and protons. Electric eels give off a kind of electricity to create a force field around themselves.

fertilizers (FUR-tuh-lize-uhrs) Fertilizers are substances that help make soil better for growing crops. Rainwater that flows into rivers can contain fertilizers.

infected (in-FEKT-ed) If something is infected, it has been contaminated with germs or viruses. A wound caused by the bite of a lamprey often gets infected.

intestines (in-TESS-tinz) Intestines are the long tubes that lead away from the stomach that are part of the digestive system. A sea cucumber can shoot its intestines out of its body when it is threatened.

krill (KRIL) Krill are tiny animals that live in the ocean. A whale can eat about 40 million krill in a day.

mucus (MYOO-kuhs) Mucus is the sticky liquid that lines the inside of your nose, throat, mouth, and some other body parts. Hagfish are known as slime eels because they are covered with mucus.

pesticides (PESS-tuh-sides) Pesticides are chemicals used to kill pests such as insects. Rainwater picks up pesticides as it runs along the ground.

plankton (PLANGK-tuhn) Plankton are microscopic plants and animals that live in water and float along with the currents. A big gulp of lake water could contain thousands of plankton.

pores (PORZ) Pores are tiny holes in the skin of an animal. Mucus oozes out of about ninety pores that line the body of a hagfish.

predator (PRED-uh-tur) A predator is an animal that hunts and eats other animals. When a hagfish wants to avoid a predator, it oozes out streams of thick, gooey mucus.

tentacles (TEN-tuh-kuhls) Tentacles are long, flexible limbs found on some living things. Jellyfish have long tentacles.

venom (VEN-uhm) Venom is poison produced in the bodies of some animals. The venom of a blue-ringed octopus can kill an adult human being in minutes.

volt (VOHLT) A volt is a unit for measuring the force of an electrical current. An electric eel can send out a 500-volt shock that is strong enough to knock over a large mammal standing in shallow water.

FOR MORE INFORMATION

Marsh, Laura. *Weird Sea Creatures.* Washington, DC: National Geographic 2012.

National Geographic Kids. *Weird But True! Ocean.* Washington, DC: National Geographic, 2021.

Ostopowich, Melanie. *Oceans Lakes and Rivers.* New York, NY: Weigl Publishers, Incorporated, 2018.

Wilsdon, Christina. *Ultimate Oceanpedia: The Most Complete Ocean Reference Ever.* Washington, DC: National Geographic 2014.

Visit our website to learn more about gross stuff underwater:
childsworld.com/links

Note to Parents, Teachers, and Librarians: We routinely verify our weblinks to make sure they are safe, active sites—so encourage your readers to check them out!

INDEX